THE ESOTERIC THOUGHTS AND WRITINGS OF OLUKEMI

DR. KENYATTA HILLS

Copper Ink Publishing, LLC

THE ESOTERIC THOUGHTS AND WRITINGS OF OLUKEMI

Contents

Dedication

Father God, I thank you. I thank you for using me as a vessel of knowledge and spiritual wisdom. Thank you, Divine Spirit of creation, for art, language, dance, music, and laughter.

Thanks to my Ancestors known and unknown for allowing me to become their prayers manifested into flesh. Thanks to the essence of Oya "The Mother of 9" the Orisha of change, transformation, and rebirth.

Thanks to my Love system: my beautiful mother Gale Shepard for encouraging me to use my talents to impact the world. To my sister Lakesha Hills, your strength and intelligence has inspired me to reveal my gifts to the world. Thanks to my niece Empress and nephew Seth for listening to me read aloud multiple essay drafts and adding a bit of humor to an already stressful writing project.

Most of all I want to thank all my supportive family and friends. Your continuous love, support, and encouragement will always be appreciated.

FOREWARD

I think of you often. I love you too. I have this rage. This rage in the pit of my stomach that I will use as a catalyst for change.

See I refuse to forget what was done to my people. My own flesh and blood. I use all that was meant for our demise as building blocks to build up my tribe.

Everything always works out. And if it doesn't, it's because it'll work out even better than you imagined.

My people, hold on!

My maternal ancestor, I will call her Sayrah. She told me in a dream, "ti o ba ti i le se o ti o le ṣe ti o", If I can do it you can do it.

She kissed me on my forehead and whispered, "Iwọ ni ohun ti a gbadura fun, duro lagbara", You are what we prayed for, stay strong.

My people, hold on!

"Untitled" poem written by Lakesha Hills

Preface

As the author of this book of opinion essays my intention is for readers to use the 18 compiled essays as a guide to understanding and embracing self-awareness, mental stillness, and spiritual evolution. As you read each essay, I ask that you process all information with a critical mind. Use cognitive flexibility and consider the different perspectives, evidence, and reasoning mentioned in the essays. The chapters of "The Esoteric Thoughts and Writings of Olukemi" is divided into "9" colors (yellow, copper, blue, gold, red, orange, green, silver, and purple). Each chapter's title has words associated with the energy of the color. For example, Chapter 9 is purple, and the words associated with the chapter are "manifestation", "imagination", and "universal flow". Chapter 5 is red, and the words associated with the chapter are "stability", "courage", and "physical/mental energy". Chapter 3 is blue, and the words associated with the chapter are "truth, "emotional depth", and "inner peace". Each chapter has two essays. The topic of each essay is connected to the color and associated words in the chapter title. For example, Chapter 2 is copper, associated words are "comfort", "abundance", and "positivity". The topics of the essays are "Cogito, Ergo Sum: I Think, Therefore I am" and "Mental Peace". Another example is Chapter 6, chapter 6 is orange, associated words are "creativity", "productivity", and "emotional expression". The topics of the essays are "Human Nature and Emotional Intelligence" and "The Power of Words".

Next, I will discuss the definition of "Esoteric" and the use of the name "Olukemi" in the title of "The Esoteric Thoughts and Writings of Olukemi". Esoteric is a type of writing that is only understood by a select few who have special knowledge or interest in what is written. Esoteric writing is also seen as a type of writing that is hermetic, abstruse, or alchemic. My opinion essays may not appeal to most, but my hope is that the select few who have esoteric interest in the topics use information learned in the essays to improve their lives and share knowledge of self-awareness with other like-minded individuals.

"Olukemi" was born summer of 2005 on the campus of University of Florida. As a liberal arts student majoring in English, I had to take "2" foreign language courses to satisfy graduation requirements. Fall 2004 and Spring of 2005 I wasted my two class withdrawals to get out of Spanish. The first time I took the course in Fall of 2004, I was clueless about what was being said and the professor spoke so fast you would have thought he was the sixth member of Bone Thugs in Harmony, "Professor Spanish Loco Bone". After 2 days of scatter brain, I decided to withdraw and try Spanish again the next semester. Spring 2005 comes around, and I am sitting in "Professor Spanish Loco Bone" class again. The professor started class by greeting each student saying "Buenos días, cómo estás hoy?" (Good morning, how are you today?). When he got around to me, my mind went blank, and I forgot what to say in response. I stood up, gathered my thoughts, and responded with "Muy Mala" (very bad). I sat back down and waited until the professor started greeting the next row of students before sneaking out the side door of the classroom. After leaving class, I went directly to the computer lab in Marston Science Library and used my last withdrawal to drop Spanish class for the second time.

I was projected to graduate at the end of summer B term in August of 2005 and had to take whatever foreign language was being offered for the upcoming summer A and B terms. The only foreign language class being offered that summer was a West African language named "Yoruba". I knew nothing of the language, but I did know I am a decedent of west African's, and a large majority may have spoken the language of Yoruba. At the end of the first day of class Dr. Akinyemi gave us a list of Yoruba names and asked that we introduce ourselves as new Yoruba names. He asked that we put thought into our names because in the Yoruba culture the name of an individual is an important aspect of that person's identity and social status. He also explained how an individual's name influences their destiny and shape their life's journey. Given the information from Dr. Akinyemi and the list of Yoruba names I decided to introduce myself as 'Olukemi' (God cares for me). I selected the name for its meaning and name bearer characteristics of being patient, strong willed, creative, a good student, and having the ability to absorb and retain knowledge easily. The next two terms consisted of "Olukemi" learning to speak and write in Yoruba and successfully passing both sections of Yoruba. 'Olukemi' graduated on time to walk in the August 2005 Summer graduation. Not only did I 'Kenyatta' walk across the stage and graduate, 'Olukemi' also walked across the stage and achieved the same milestone as I.

Esoteric writers who inspired essay topics in this book are:

- Ralph Waldo Emerson ("The Transcendentalist"; "Self-Reliance"; and "The Over-Soul")
- William Walker Atkinson ("The Secret of the I AM"; "The Law of Attraction"; and "Essential Prosperity")
- Florance Scovel Shinn ("The Game of Life & How to Play it"; "Your Word is your Wand"; and "The Magic Path of Intuition")
- Nepoleon Hill ("Think and Grow Rich"; "The Psychology of Wealth"; and "Dream Big")
- Neville Goddard ("Your Faith is your Fortune"; "The Power of Awareness"; and "Awakened Imagination")

There are two essays I will discuss in more detail: 1) "Imagination: The Superpower of Storytelling"; 2) "Human Nature and Emotional Intelligence"

The essay "Imagination: The Superpower of Storytelling" was inspired by the writings of Zora Neal Hurston. Hurston was a world-renowned African American author, anthropologist, folklorist, and influential member of the Harlem Renaissance. She used her research and extensive travels through the American South and Caribbean to write numerous novels including "Mules and Men", "Their Eyes Were Watching God", "Tell My Horse", and "Spunk". In the essay "Imagination:

The Superpower of Storytelling" its mentioned, "The nature of story-telling explores the highs and lows of human life using language and expression to communicate ideas, opinions, behaviors, and beliefs". In comparison to the works of Hurston and the topic of imagination, not only did Hurston use research and travel experiences as inspiration for her writings, but she also used her imagination". It's mentioned in the essay that "the human mind is where one's personal narrative uses the gift of imagination...Imagination plays a key role in storytelling". Inspirational quotes from Zora Neal Hurston and J.G Ballard was used to support the topic of the essay.

The essay "Human Nature and Emotional Intelligence" connects the nature of humans, human evolution, emotions and the use of emotional intelligence to console individuals in emotional situations. Its mentioned how "humans are unique beings" and how humans have evolved from Homo Habilis (able man) and Homo Sapien (wise man). Advancements of "able man" is the mental ability to perform a task. Advancements of "wise man" is the mental intellect to investigate, de-velop, and create meaning of life experiences". It further discussed how life experiences are driven by emotional reactions. In the essay it men-tioned how an "individual's spiritual sense of love have the potential to provide reassurance in an emotional situation". It goes on to discuss how, "emotions have the potential to be enlightening and powerful" and those same emotions can be "regulated and understood using emotional intelligence". Inspirational quotes from Deepak Chopra and Adam Grant was used to support the topic of the essay.

As a final word, before you begin Chapter 1: Yellow "Intuition, Personal Power, and Enlightenment", may I provide a brief suggestion. Read with an open mind and focus on the purpose of each essay to "convey a great universal truth which all who are ready may learn, not only what to do, but also how to do it, and receive, as well, the needed stimulus to make a start" (Hill, 1937).

Dr. Kenyatta Hills

Yellow: Intuition, Personal Power, and Enlightenment

Believing and Knowing

The human mind has the capability to separate and recognize an individual's reason, instinct, perception, belief, and knowledge. The distinction between "belief" and "knowledge" is that our knowledge, experiences, memories, and senses help validate our beliefs. The words "belief" and "knowledge" are terms used in our society that can potentially have different usages depending on how the terms are being expressed (Halla, 2018). My personal definition of "belief" is the use of ideals and traditional practices to connect with an entity with the intentions to fully believe. For example, "belief" can be utilized to verify many personalized truths to help generate a sense of approval or acceptance. An individual may believe an inflated balloon will remain full of air without accepting the fact the balloon has the potential to lose air pressure due to time and wear of the balloon material. Acceptance of a belief requires further inquiry and clarity to make the belief real and relatable to oneself and others.

The term "knowledge" is defined as a specific belief that is justified to be true and concrete. Knowledge generates a sense of power and strength in one's belief system (Halla, 2018). A great number of individuals in our society are willing to accept an idea without evidence to support their acceptance of the belief. Mental conflict occurs when one's beliefs, values, perspectives, and attitudes are tested. For example, if one's beliefs are challenged with false assumptions, it's important that the individual reevaluates their beliefs with information to minimize mental conflict. Knowledge is vital to sustaining an individual's moral practices and intentions (Halla, 2018). Without knowledge, one's belief system has the potential to become unstable.

Inspirational Quotes:

- Believers can ask God for more knowledge (**Psalm 119:66**).
- "Believing is not the same as knowing. Believing is second-hand knowledge, whereas knowing is first-hand experience. When your action comes from a level of belief, there is fear, doubt, and restlessness behind such action. When your action comes from a level of knowing, there is conviction, certainty, and calm behind such action."- **Yogi Kanna, Nirvana : Absolute Freedom**

Intuition verses Ego

The world we live in values power. It's all about power, dominance, and control. Intuition is true power. Intuition is regarded as an internal power (Nado, 2014). Intuition plays a powerful role in one's spiritual development. We must be willing to pay attention to the still internal voice of our intuition. Valuing our internal intuition makes it easier to receive healing, peace, and an unlimited number of blessings.

The illusion the ego projects is of strength, but its weak in nature. The ego flexes its muscles and throws its weight around. The ego is to blame for issues between individuals and nations. The ego feeds off the energy of corruption, violence, manipulation, and deception. Intuition and ego will remain opposing forces until we learn to conquer our ego and demand submission to our internal intuition (Poag, 2022).

Our intuition perceives beyond the physical senses and all universal activities (Nado, 2014). It is independent of matter and doesn't need recognition to exist. Spiritual clarity and obedience to your internal intuition has the potential to save oneself from spiritual limbo and realign with creation.

Inspirational Quotes:

- "Messages from the ego are driven by self-interest. When intuition is pure, it is not motivated by self-preservation or fear. That means that unselfish intuition feels different in your body – it feels open, light, and relaxed, not constricted."- **Deepak Chopra**
- "Trusting your intuition means tuning in as deeply as you can to the energy you feel, following that energy moment to moment, trusting that it will lead you where you want to go and bring you everything you desire." - **Shakti Gawain**

CHAPTER TWO

Copper: Comfort, Abundance, and Positivity

Energy is Currency

Energy is the currency of life. Our lives and the world around us function from the use of energy. Energy cannot be destroyed, but it can be manipulated. The infinite amount of universal energy is what keeps us alive and thriving (Martinez, 2023; Vallis, 2021). In our lives we are given an infinite amount of energy. How and where we invest our energy determines an individual's overall life purpose. The existence of energy can't be captured with the human physical eye. Energy is an unseen force that binds onto everything inside and outside of our physical reality whether we acknowledge it or not (Martinez, 2023). If energy is currency, we must recognize how much energy we must keep to ourselves or share with selected individuals.

An individual must be selective in how they use their energy. The energy of our thoughts is different from the energy in our blood and organs. The human body produces different levels of energy currency. Energy is neither good nor bad, it depends on the perception of the individual experiencing the energy force (Hareesh, 2015). It's important to pay attention to your energy. Energy acts as a strong connection between your 'oneness' and the 'collective' universal consciousness. Allowing your consciousness to focus on an individual or event that infuriates you provides the entity with your energy, and that same energy reciprocates the experience of being infuriated.

If you are poor in energy currency, the first step is to affirm yourself rich in energy. You can increase value to your energy reserve by thinking and speaking more positively. The second step is to pay more attention to your breathing by inhaling slowly from your diaphragm to help transfer energy and fresh oxygen to your brain and other parts of your body. The third step is to take 5 to 10 minutes out of your day to use your energy to silently imagine turning challenges into successful outcomes.

You can also use energy to imagine the kind of positive life experiences your heart desires and deserves. Where you invest your energy is the most important choice for living a fulfilled life (Martinez, 2023; Vallis, 2021). Your energy is your treasured, nonrefundable currency and your time is your secure investment (Hareesh, 2015). Wisely invest your energy my friends and remember to keep your energy reserve full.

Inspirational Quotes:

- "Energy is the currency of the universe. When you 'pay' attention to something, you 'buy' into that experience."- **Emily Maroutian**
- " Energy is the only universal currency: one of its many forms must be transformed to another for stars to shine, planets to rotate, plants to grow, and civilizations to evolve."-**Vaclav Smil**

Mental Peace

Our minds are conditioned to stay mentally busy. We often neglect giving our mind rest and relaxation. Mental peace is something we humans long for but fail to find. Failure to find mental peace is due to us seeking peace in things that provide temporary satisfaction (Bourtos, 2024; Chérif et al., 2022). The enjoyment or contentment from things that give short-lived satisfaction will only sustain an individual long enough to release stress or frustration until they are once again searching for mental peace. Mental peace is freeing your mind from the restraints of life and all disturbing thoughts and emotions (Moore, 2019).

Mental peace is having dominion over oneself to not only satisfy their mind but your entire being. This can be done by knowing the difference between fictitious mental peace (money, appeasing others, or a well-functioning Government) and authentic mental peace (love, joy, or contentment). Without a true understanding of money an individual may think their peace will come from monetary means, but without discipline and money knowledge the anticipated "peace" can turn into "anguish" or "grief". Another example is gaining peace by appeasing others. Many of us are so unsure of ourselves we tend to seek peace by appeasing others in our homes and jobs. Appeasing others is a sure-fire way to lose your power to experience personal peace for yourself.

Gaining mental peace can be created in a few different ways: 1) meditation; 2) developing love for yourself; 3) surround yourself with positive people; 4) cultivate a positive mindset; 5) practice gratitude; 6) practice deep conscious breathing using the "4, 6, 8 deep breathing method"; and 7) visualization of a peaceful place (mental escape) to foster inner peace. When my life gets funky, I find mental peace using the following "5" methods: 1) deep conscious breathing [to clear my mind and release unwanted energy]; 2) meditation [connect with myself mentally and spiritually]; 3) spending time with positive people; 4) the practice of gratitude (to God and my Ancestors); and 5) developing love for myself. As a proactive exercise create a list of the "5" methods you would like to implement into your life. Once the "5" methods are consistently implemented, you will start to experience mental peace within yourself and when dealing with others. Remember "mental peace" puts your life at ease.

Inspirational Quotes:

- "You find peace not by rearranging the circumstances of your life, but by realizing who you are at the deepest level."- **Eckhart Tolle**
- "Nothing can bring you peace but yourself." -**Ralph Waldo Emerson**

Blue: Truth, Emotional Depth, and Inner Peace

Freedom of Truth

During an EI (Emotional Intelligence) coaching session, one of my clients stated, "I'm no longer a people pleaser. I remembered who I am and started living in my truth". Her statement prompted me to do an in-depth analysis of the term "truth" and how her beliefs and values impact what she believes to be her mental and spiritual "truth"? The understanding of our truths come from sources beyond what is physically seen. In definition, truth is the reality of a person's logic aligned with their individual perspectives of life experiences (Wyatt et al., 2022). Values set our standards of what we think is important (Lonscu, 2022). If one's beliefs are things seen as being true, values become a life compass providing direction to what is wrong or right (Lonscu, 2022). Beliefs and values also shape an individual's mental and spiritual truth. Knowledge of "truth" redeems us and brings our true self in alignment with the Divine. Based on how one's beliefs and values direct their "truth", living in one's "truth" helps awaken oneself to reconnect with knowing who they are mentally and spiritually. According to Martin Heidegger (1943), "The essence of truth reveals itself as freedom... what is initially and generally admitted as being known and giving a sense of unfamiliarity". Over time that same sense of unfamiliar freedom transforms into a level of freedom that allow individuals to use beliefs and values to define their "truth" and freely live without judgement or limitations. Doing so gives us freedom to discern the truth from lies, gain strength to withstand negativity, and consciously eliminate the enemy's veil of deception and manipulation.

Inspirational Quotes:

- "Truth has a power only the courageous can handle." – **Anthon St. Maarten**
- "I remembered who I am. And that changed everything"- **Spoken word poem by Laurel Dewey**

Inner Silence

Inner silence is not just a form of muting distracting noises and thoughts. Inner silence is a place of refuge when we need to escape the harsh realities of life's pressures (Center for Action & Contemplation, 2020). We are safe in the presence of our inner silence. Inner silence frees us from the clatter and commotion of the world (Sri Sri Ravi Shankar, 2016). Inner silence generates a level of peace that surpasses all tranquility and sereneness. What makes inner silence special is how we experience its authentic peace and stillness. The energy of inner silence permeates the part of our soul that craves stillness. In stillness, mind chatter quiet, thought clouds clear away, and the star of awareness illuminates an individual's oneness (Sri Sri Ravi Shankar, 2016). Only in our inner silence will our truths be revealed. When focusing on our inner silence and becoming a silent observer, all truth becomes self-evident without the need for proof or explanation. Eckhart Tolle stated "In the stillness, the truth becomes apparent. When thoughts subside, the truth of your being emerges as pure Aliveness — Presence — Awareness" (Tolle, 2023). Within the atmosphere of inner silence dwells pure conviction. This high level of conviction strips away all blemishes and restores the feeling of peace. We can explore the deepest phases of inner silence by closing one's eyes, breathing in deep, and tuning into the silence of the mind. Once tapped into the mental space of inner silence, an individual can potentially experience complete detachment from all negative energy allowing the soul to experience complete rest.

Inspirational Quotes:

- "In the silence, we can hear the whispers of our soul." – **Deepak Chopra**

- "Silence is the language of God; all else is poor translation."
  – **Rumi**

Gold: Divinity, Generosity, and Success

Soul Responsibility

Every human being on planet Earth has a soul. The human soul is our vehicle for multi and interdimensional exchanges of energy. Once the human soul is created, its energy exists forever. The soul is the spiritual part of a human that gives life to the body (Desai, 2021). It's the non-material essence of an individual (identity, memories, personality, etc.). One of the most serious responsibilities entrusted to a human being is the possession of its soul. Soul responsibility is being aware that you have a soul and becoming conscious of the responsibility to protect your soul regardless of life experiences (Spinks, n.d.). The power of soul responsibility is measured by an individual's conscious elements of perceptions, ideas, and emotions. Soul responsibility recognizes the value of the human soul (Spinks, n.d.). The value of the human soul cannot be calculated. There are billions upon billions of human souls, all created by God, but each soul is unique and worth more than anti-matter, diamonds, or gold. Individuals who are unaware of their soul's value become neglectful and irresponsible with their lives. Neglectfulness and lack of responsibility makes the souls of men easy pickings for the unjustifiable appetite of the enemy. The enemy loves when we endanger our souls with malice behavior, envy, and resentment to harden our hearts. The enemy deserves to starve and nawl on his own bones. Suit up for battle and protect your soul at all costs.

Inspirational Quotes:

- "Responsibility is good for your soul."-**Judah Smith**
- "The soul is responsible for our thoughts, emotions, and desires."-**Aristotle 'On The Soul'**

Nuturing your Internal Divinity

We are divine beings. To be divine means to be of God; heavenly; superb or magically powerful. Nurturing our internal divinity produces unlimited amounts of harmony. Nurturing your internal divinity consist of nourishing your spirit (Turner, n.d.). Nourishment comes in many forms. Reading the right literature can open your mind to receiving access to more nourishing and spiritual stimulating information. Applying newly learned spiritual knowledge enhances your life and awaken your internal divinity (Wixom, 2015). One way to awaken your internal divinity is to feed it (Mashburn, 2020). Feed it with nourishing positive energy, bible verses, spiritual motivating quotes, and interactions with other believers of God. Paying more attention to your internal divinity is the first step into reaching your full potential. You must acknowledge your internal divinity and remain mindful every day of the strength you receive from nurturing and spending time with your internal divine spirit.

Inspirational Quotes:

- "Your inner voice is the voice of divinity. To hear it, we need to be in solitude, even in crowded places."-**A. R. Rahman**
- "Trust and value your own divinity as well as your connection to nature. Seeing God's work everywhere will be your reward."-**Wayne Dyer**

CHAPTER FIVE

Red: Intention, Thought, and Victory

Cogito, Ergo Sum: I Think, Therefore I am

The ancestor of every action is a thought. The most challenging task for humans is to ponder important questions and remain open to new ideas and forms of thinking. Every action is generated in the mind from a thought. Thoughts have the power to hinder personal progress and growth (Lewis, 2023). Thoughts become things once we give energy to their growth. Depending on the intentions of the person, energy projected by thoughts can be used to manifest focused thoughts into reality (Miller, 2004). One must become aware of the influence "thinking" has on one's life. According to René Descartes' philosophical statement "Cogito ergo sum" (I think, therefore I am), Descartes stated that "our thoughts are limited to our current state of consciousness" (Maden, 2023). To be a conscious thinker one must have knowledge of their true selves as a 'human energy conductor'. Understanding is accomplished by using one's energy, focus, and conscious thinking to manifest a specific outcome or experience into reality. Knowing who you are as a 'human energy conductor' and having a direct connection with the great "I am", you have the power to manifest any and everything you desire into your life. In the New Testament, Jesus presented himself in the following manifestation titles of "I Am": "*I am* the bread of life" (John 6:35); "*I am* the vine" (John 15:15); and "*I am* the way the truth and the life" (John 14:6). Each manifestation title Jesus called himself starts with "I am" as a conscious thought of who and what he is as the incarnate of God. It's a great idea for individuals to see themselves as "I am" in their thoughts and play them out in action. For example, a few "I am" titles I use to help navigate life's challenges are: "*I am* strong"; "*I am* at peace"; "*I am* favored"; "*I am* head strong"; and "*I am* healthy and wealthy". These titles give me confidence and reassurance of who

"I am" as a creation of God. Two main phrases of "I am" I use daily are "*I am* disciplined during times of temptation" and "*I am* abundance during times of lack". Individuals who declare, believe, and act "I am" into their lives have the power to manifest positive experiences into reality.

Inspirational Quotes:

- "The world as we have created it is a process of thinking. It cannot be changed without changing our thinking." -**Albert Einstein**
- "The key to success is to focus our conscious mind on things we desire not things we fear."-**Brian Tracy**

Battle of the Spirit

Right now, you and I are in the middle of a war, a spiritual war. Every one of us are in a continuous fight with our fleshly desires. It's a daily battle, and sadly, our society is full of carnal worldly influences. Scripture explains the Spirit wars against the flesh and the flesh wars against the Spirit, so they are continually hostile toward one another. It's a war! The enemy hates us and is constantly working overtime to destroy us. His goal is to manipulate us to act on our fleshly desires. For example, I find strength from dedicating time to meditating on spiritual affirmations by Florence Scovel Shinn. The first spiritual affirmation is "Divine order is now established in my mind, body, and affairs. I see clearly and act quickly and my greatest expectations come to pass in a miraculous way" (Shinn, 2016). The second affirmation is "All that is mine by Divine Right is now released and reaches me in great avalanches of abundance, under grace in miraculous ways" (Shinn, 2016). Take time to consciously focus on the meaning of each word, how each word makes you feel, and how applying each affirmation's energy to your life help create a vision of victory against the enemy.

Inspirational Quotes:

- "It is important to remember that you should pick and choose your battles. Sometimes, what appears to be a battle to some is really a victory for you, especially when you don't engage in hostile and aggressive actions. That is important. Rise above. Maintain your dignity. Remember, the battle is God's. He won't abandon you."-**June Stoyer**
- "Spiritual warfare is very real. There is a furious, fierce, and ferocious battle raging in the realm of the spirit between the forces

of God and the forces of evil. Warfare happens every day, all the time. Whether you believe it or not, you are in a battlefield. You are in warfare." -**Pedro Okoro**

CHAPTER SIX

Orange: Creativity, Productivity, and Emotional Expression

Human Nature and Emotional Intelligence

Humans are unique beings. The meaning of our existence and life purpose has pondered the minds of many for centuries. Human evolution has scientifically proved how humans have advanced from being an "able man" (Homo Habilis) to a "wise man" (Homo Sapien). The name "able man" refers to a human who possesses the necessary physical capability and mental capacity to perform a task (Meinch, 2023). The meaning of "wise man" refers to a human who possess the capability to use mental intellect when investigating, developing, and creating meaning of life experiences (Groeneveld, 2017). Imagine being a "wise man" looking up into the sky and wondering what are those tiny things sparkling? Why is that big shiny orange thing rising out of the ground, moving across the sky, and back down into the ground? Who am I? why am I here? After centuries of human evolution and expansion one main question that still ponders the minds of many is "why do I feel this way"?

Feelings are reactions from our five basic human senses. Feelings are generated from what we see, smell, hear, taste, and touch. The reactions of those 5 senses help to create what we know as "Emotions". Emotions have the potential to be enlightening and powerful. And where there is enlightenment and power, there is also great responsibility. Those same powerful emotions can be regulated and understood using emotional intelligence (Cherry, 2024). A child may love their mother so much that the child displays anger and sadness when separated from their mother's comfort. The child is displaying the basics of emotional intelligence. Emotions can be expressed in the forms of joy, pain, sadness, and love.

Emotional intelligence (EI) is the cognitive ability to regulate, use, and maintain one's emotions. The practice of emotional intelligence has the potential to enlighten individuals in the areas of healthy self-emotional management, adaptation to changing circumstances, understanding the emotions of others, and maintaining positive social relationships (Cherry, 2024). An individual's spiritual sense of love have the potential to console and provide reassurance in an emotional situation. The most powerful emotion all humans desire is to spiritually and physically feel and express love. If not properly understood, the emotion of love can be detrimental to an individual's self-love 'oneness' and their love group 'collective'. An individual may express their love 'oneness' for roses, but do they love roses enough to allow the bush to bloom an abundance of roses for all 'collective' to enjoy and love. We as "wise men" should consider using the knowledge of emotional intelligence along with our capability to use mental intellect when creating meaning and cultivating a stronger understanding of EI and how to process emotions. This should be done not only for our own emotional development but the emotional development of future generations of "wise men".

Inspirational Quotes:

- When emotional intelligence merges with spiritual intelligence, human nature is transformed." -**Deepak Chopra**
- Some of the greatest moments in human history were fueled by emotional intelligence. -**Adam Grant**

The Power of Words

Every word we speak has power. Words have the power to bless as well as curse. Words have the power to build or destroy empires, bring delight or despair, or to heal or crush one's spirit. God's Word says that death and life are in the power of the tongue. Most people, when they desperately want something, will say things like, "I am dying for that piece of cake!" Few will say, "I am living for that piece of cake!". Life frustrations may cause someone to say, "I'm sick and tired of this mess", them not knowing that the words they are speaking can manifest low energy, sickness, and other health related issues into their lives. Instead of speaking sickness and death, say, "I will live long and not die young". Stop giving energy into speaking lack and poverty, use your energy to declare that "God's Word tells us all good things are already here...pronounce your life blessed" (Prince, 2024). Pronounce your life successful and fruitful. Declare darkness and pain, poverty and sorrow, defeat, and depression, will not be in your life" (Prince, 2024). Instead of speaking fear over your children, declare, "God's Word proclaims that the seed of the righteous shall be delivered. Therefore, my children are delivered from every curse, all power of darkness and evil. I call forth a prosperous, bright, and pleasant future for my children" (Prince, 2024). God wants you to have a life filled with magnificent days and an overflow of every good thing. Remember the power of your word creates your reality.

Inspirational Quotes:

- "Death and life are in the power of the tongue, and those who love it will eat its fruit" -**Proverbs 18:21**

- "Words are the most powerful thing in the universe... Words are containers. They contain faith, or fear, and they produce after their kind."-**Charles Capps**

CHAPTER SEVEN

Green : Balance, Stability, and Energy

CTRL + ALT + DEL:
Balance of Emotions

Emotional balance is something we all should seek to establish in our lives. Most individuals fail to maintain balance because of their lack of knowledge and understanding of their emotions. Emotions are how we authentically feel about things. We all experience both enjoyable and unexciting feelings. Emotional balance is the ability to balance pleasant and unpleasant feelings to generate a positive mental wellbeing. Daniel Goldman stated, "individuals who are emotional balanced (emotional self-control) has the ability to remain calm and clear-headed during a stressful event." Learning to positively maintain balance is a healthy way to establish emotional stability. Along with understanding how to maintain balance comes an in-depth comprehension of how emotional stability serves as a guiding principle for living a purposeful and successful life.

When experiencing my own personal challenges (hormonal imbalance, stress, depression, and anxiety) of maintaining emotional balance and stability, I practice what I named "CTRL + ALT + DEL life reset method". I created the life reset method for my clients who are learning to recognize and balance their emotions. Practicing the CTRL + ALT + DEL life reset method reminds an individual to take control of how they are emotionally feeling. The method also allow the individual time to mentally reset, alter, or delete emotions that no longer serve their life purpose. The CTRL + ALT + DEL life reset method follows the following steps:

- CTRL (Control): Acknowledge what you are feeling, take 3 deep breaths, allow yourself to feel what you are feeling (emotions), and exhaling release of control to God.

- ALT (Alternate): Recognize how releasing control to God alters your heart, mind, spirit, and your way of living.
- DEL (Delete): Let go of old thought patterns and emotions that generate doubt, depression, confusion, or anxiety. Allow God to restore deleted emotions with feelings of peace, growth, purpose, and success in your life.

Individuals who practice the CTRL + ALT + DEL life reset method and apply it to their lives become more mentally and emotionally balanced in their relationships, careers, and life in general.

Inspirational Quotes:

- "When you let go of what you can't control, true peace can then enter your life. This is the path to achieving emotional balance."- **Shannon L. Alder**
- "No person, place, or thing has any power over us, for 'we' are the only thinkers in our mind. When we create peace and harmony and balance in our minds, we will find it in our lives."- **Louise L. Hay**

Beta Brain Waves: Frequency of Thought

The human brain is an electrochemical organ. A fully functioning human brain can generate as much as 10 watts of electrical power (Kotsos, 2021). According to researcher, Ned Herrmann, "even though this electrical power is very limited, it does occur in very specific ways that are characteristic of the human brain." Herrmann continued to explain how electrical activity and hormones released by the brain is displayed in the form of brainwaves. Beta brainwaves are generated when the human brain is aroused and actively engaged in conscious mental activities. Beta brain waves function at frequency between 12-30 Hertz (Kotsos, 2021). Beta brain waves are traits of a strongly engaged mind that thrives on mental stimulation. A person in active conversation, a debater making a rebuttal response, or a teacher would be functioning in beta waves when they are engaged in the mental activities of their work. Adults who constantly operate at high levels of Beta brainwaves during their awake hours experience thoughts of stress, anxiousness, and restlessness (Kotsos, 2021). For example, when Beta brainwaves are functioning at a normal frequency the brain consciously experience the inner 'voice' of logic, critical reasoning, and discernment. The opposite occurs when Beta brainwaves are functioning at an elevated or high frequency. A human brain functioning at high Beta brainwaves experience the inner 'voice' of constant and often negative invasive chatter that become louder during times of heightened stress.

The human brain functioning in Beta brainwaves has an impact on how emotional experiences, triggers, and memories are processed. When I conduct lectures on emotional intelligence and the human brain, I provide a clear explanation of how emotions are processed in 3 main brain areas: 1) Brain Stem & Cerebellum (instinctual brain);

2) Limbic (emotional brain); 3) Neocortex (logic brain). For example, if the human brain is functioning at an elevated Beta brain wave frequency the stressful situation triggers the instinctual brain region into autopilot (instinctive behaviors) to protect, defend, or freeze. The high jacking of the instinctual brain into autopilot, based on stressful triggers generated in the emotional brain produce negative feelings, tension, and behaviors. The high jacking blocks the logic brain from using effective reasoning, communication, and self-control to minimize negative expressions of emotions (Hills, 2022).

In other words, Beta brain waves functioning at an elevated or heightened frequency has a direct relation to how negative emotional triggers are processed in the human brain. Regular meditation, exercise, deep breathing, and closed-eye visualization techniques help boost creativity, release of serotonin and endorphins, and increase relaxation to promote balanced beta brain waves (Meda, 2020). The next time you feel tight, stressed, overstimulated, or triggered, think about balancing your Beta brain waves, and what you can do to calm your brain and boost your mental energy.

Inspirational Quotes:

- "The human brain is a complex organ with the wonderful power of enabling man to find reasons for continuing to believe whatever it is that he wants to believe."- **Voltaire**
- "Every human brain is both a broadcasting and receiving station for the vibration of thought."-**Napoleon Hill**

CHAPTER EIGHT

Silver: Evolution, Gratitude, and Consciousness

Human Consciousness:
The Idea of Self-Awareness

Human consciousness is the awareness of oneself in society and the world around them. Awareness covers the totality of what it is to be conscious (Voice of America, 2023). Conscious self-awareness is associated with a more complex thought process. This level of awareness is subjective and unique to each person. If you describe something you are personally experiencing (grief, joy, gratitude, etc.) in words, then what you are experiencing is part of a more complex thought process (consciousness) (Cherry, 2023; Thrineshwara, 2018). Individuals who are consciously self-aware are open to expressing their vulnerability to others. Those individuals gain trust from others via the use of transparency and aren't concerned with being judged or rejected. Self-aware individuals are also equipped with unique behaviors, thoughts, and emotions to aid in personal growth (Cherry, 2023; Thrineshwara, 2018). Those same individuals are fully aware of who they are as a person and in society.

Human consciousness also requires attention. Attention is the focal point of concentration by an individual (Biswas-Diener & Teeny, 2024). Focusing attention on one specific thing provides a distorted view of reality, especially if the focus is on what is negatively happening at the current moment. Those who are self-aware possess the following skills and abilities (Chowdhury, 2023; Biswas-Diener & Teeny, 2024; Voice of America, 2023):

- Objectively evaluate their thoughts, emotions, and behaviors
- Manage their emotions (positive and negative)
- Align their actions with their values
- Gain a clear understanding of how others perceive them

- Gain a strong understanding of what they emotionally need
- Use their self-awareness to reduce stress and minimize anxious thoughts and behaviors

Implementing the above skills and abilities help strengthen an individual's conscious self-awareness in society.

Inspirational Quotes:

- "Our greatest human adventure is the evolution of consciousness. We are in this life to enlarge the soul, liberate the spirit, and light up the brain."-**Tom Robbins 'Wild Ducks Flying Backwards'**
- "Human consciousness and universal consciousness are in reality one and the same."-**Muata Ashby 'The Egyptian Book of the Dead'**

Spiritual Evolution, Gratitude, and Growth

Spiritual gratitude is the ultimate form of spiritual evolution. Expressing gratitude is the key to connecting the dots in our spiritual experience. Showing gratitude, appreciation, and reverence towards our universal creator transforms us from intellectual animals to spiritual human beings (Kang, 2015). Spiritual evolution doesn't register to the material mind because the material mind has not evolved into a higher degree of spiritual thinking (Gordon-Mead, 2023). Focus and reflection help provide understanding of spiritual evolution and the act of gratitude. When a person see themselves growing spiritually it inspires a sense of gratitude. The more you show gratitude, the more you will spiritually evolve and grow.

Inspirational Quotes:

- "Gratitude unlocks the fullness of life. It turns what we have into enough, and more. It turns denial into acceptance, chaos to order, confusion to clarity. Gratitude can turn a meal into a feast, a house into a home, a stranger into a friend. Gratitude makes sense of our past, brings peace for today and creates a vision for tomorrow." -**Melody Beattie**
- "It is through gratitude for the present moment that the spiritual dimension of life opens up." -**Eckhart Tolle**

Purple: Manifestation, Imagination, and Universal Flow

The Power of Manifestation

The concept of manifestation has been around a while, but it has become much more popular in recent years (Lazor, 2022). With the correct intentions, manifestation is the idea that you can think a positive outcome into your life by simply "claiming" it as your own and believing it will happen (Davis, 2023; Lazor, 2022). The power of manifestation is the product of successful progressive thinking. The process of progressive thinking encourages individuals to embrace the use of their human senses to manifest what they want in their lives (Scott, 1908). If you have a deep desire to own a sports car, you will start to progressively focus your energy on speaking and visualizing how the sports car will look in your driveway, the color, the new car smell, or the sound of the engine. Before long, you will start to see more sports cars in traffic, in the parking lot of the mall, advertisements on social media, and TV commercials. Consistently focusing your energy into thinking, speaking, and visualizing the ownership of the sports car adds power to making what you desire into reality. That same energy and focus can be applied to manifest other desires.

The bible talks about manifestation in several places. Manifestation is having faith and believing that God will bless you. In Genesis, we see the story of Abraham and Sarah manifesting a child even though they were very old (Boomplay, 2023). In Matthew, we read of Jesus manifesting food for the five thousand. In Philippians, Paul tells us to meditate on whatever is true, honorable, just, pure, lovely, commendable, excellent, and worthy of praise (Boomplay, 2023). All these examples show us that manifestation is a real and powerful thing that happens when we focus our thoughts and energy on something of interest. It is good practice for believers to learn to focus thoughts and energy to align their wants and desires with God's will. Manifestation stories in the bible worth reading to help give your faith a boost are: "Abraham and Isaac"; "Daniel in the Lion's Den"; "The Burning Bush"; and "Jesus healing the Blind Man".

Below are a few things to do and not to do while reading bible verses and practicing manifestation (Tarrants, 2019):

1. Read biblical passages with an open mind.
2. Pray to God for understanding of the passage you are reading.
3. Read selected passages at a slow and careful pace.
4. Discuss the passages with an individual who is knowledgeable of the Bible to minimize confusion of the word.
5. Keep a detailed journal of your Spiritual revelations, thoughts, ideas, and feelings while reading key bible verses.
6. Refrain from approaching the Bible with a "I already know everything" mindset.
7. Don't give up if you don't understand what you have read.
8. Don't forget to have fun in the process of reading bible verses and practicing manifestation.

Inspiration Quotes:

- ""The universe conspires with those who dare to manifest their desires." – **Paulo Coelho, 'The Alchemist'**
- "See it, Touch it, Obtain it" — **Demetrius and Terry Flenory, 'BMF: Season 1, Episode 1'**

Imagination: The Superpower of Storytelling

Storytelling is used as an expression of life that helps an individual make sense of life experiences. God gave humans the power and ability to construct stories that uses the power of love and truth to craft unique masterpieces of art. The use of music, words, and dance can generate a colorful story describing, explaining, and justifying one's emotional reactions and points of view (Serrat, 2008). Storytelling was created using what I call our "universal reality". Our universal reality sets the foundation for developing one's personal narrative. The nature of storytelling explores the highs and lows of human life using language and expression to communicate ideas, opinions, behaviors, and beliefs (Serrat, 2008). Storytelling has its positives and negatives of explaining human experiences based on belief. Believing and defending what is not based on truth results in negative expression of one's story. Believing and defending what is based on truth results in goodness and positive expression of one's story.

Imagination plays a key role in storytelling. The human mind is where one's personal narrative uses the gift of imagination. One of the greatest gifts God has given us is the gift of imagination (St. Aubin, 2021). It allows an individual to dream, breathe, and be fully present in its creative beauty. Imagination create situations, experiences, and events that impact and shape human consciousness (Bodo, 2023). A few examples of the act of imagination is acting, singing, playing music, and daydreaming. Most grew up participating in imaginative play with siblings and friends. Imagination allows children to explore the world around them and use their minds to create new ways of making sense of their experiences.

It's been said that one's imagination can be a breeding ground for ill intentions and evil thoughts. The bible tells us that God created the entire universe using the energy of imagination. According to 2 Corinthians 10:5, "Cast down imaginations that go against the knowledge of God, and bring into captivity every thought that is obedient to Christ". It's the responsibility of the individual to use their imaginations as a source and foundation of truth, growth, and enlightenment. One must deliberately formulate a positive imaginative approach to understanding life that generates truth, love, self-discovery. We all have free will to think what we want without limits to how we can use our God-given imaginations to create some of the best experiences and stories told in the history of man (Gosetti-Ferencei, 2023). We should use storytelling and imagination as a superpower to fix our thoughts on heavenly things. Doing so reminds us to focus on values and eternal truths that will open the flood gates to receiving abundant blessings and riches far greater than imagined.

Inspirational Quotes:

- "Our stories, unique to our own lives, are not merely trivial fragments but powerful narratives that deserve to be voiced."- **Zora Neal Hurston**
- "I believe in the power of the imagination to remake the world, to release the truth within us, to hold back the night, to transcend death, to charm motorways, to ingratiate ourselves with birds, to enlist the confidences of madmen."- **G. Ballard**

About The Author

Dr. Kenyatta Hills

Dr. Hills is a native of Florida, an educator, author, entrepreneur, and speaker. Dr. Hills is a proud member of Zeta Phi Beta Sorority, Inc. She is a graduate of the University of Florida and earned her Doctorate in Business Administration specializing in Social Impact Management from Walden University.

Dr. Hills taught high school English and currently teaches university level undergraduate/graduate business courses in management, leadership strategies, organizational behavior, emotional intelligence, business communication, and human resource management. She is the owner and operator of three businesses: 1) DH Research and Consulting; 2) Klarity in Motion Emotional Coaching; and 3) Copper Ink Publishing. In 2015, she published her doctoral dissertation on "Communication Strategies to Generate Employee Job Satisfaction". Dr. Hills is an academic contributor and one of three chief editors for the international book "Multi-Disciplinary Perspectives in Thought Leadership" (2022).

In her spare time, Dr. Hills enjoys caring for her house plants, reading science fiction and afrofuturistic novels, writing, researching, resting, and spending time with family and friends. The Book "The Thoughts and Writings of Olukemi" is Dr. Hills' first published book of essays.

Dr. Hills can be contacted via email at **kenyattahills@gmail.com**

Chapter 1: Yellow "Intuition, Personal Power, and Enlightenment"

Believing is Knowing:

Halla, K. (2018). Kant and Fichte on Belief and Knowledge, Revista de Estud(i)os sobre Fichte. DOI: https://doi.org/10.4000/ref.895

Spurgeon, C. (2016). Psalm 119 Verses 65-72. https://www.blueletter-bible.org/Comm/spurgeon_charles/tod/ps119_065-072.cfm

Yogi, K. (2011). Nirvana: Absolute Freedom. Kamath Publishing.

Intuition verses Ego:

Chopra, D. (2021). Intuition and Ego. https://www.deepakchopra.com/articles/intuition-and-ego-2/

Earlenbaugh, J. & Molyneux, B. (2009). Intuitions are Inclinations to Believe. Philosophical Studies, 145(1): 89–109. Doi:10.1007/s11098-009-9388-4

Gawain, S. (n.d.). PassItOn. https://www.passiton.com/inspirational-quotes/3502-trusting-your-intuition-means-tuning-in-as

Nado, J. (2014). Why Intuition. Philosophy and Phenomenological Research, 89(1): 15–41. Doi:10.1111/j.1933-1592.2012.00644.x

Poag, M. (2022). The True Nature of the Ego, and How it Destroys your Life. https://www.linkedin.com/pulse/true-nature-ego-how-destroys-your-life-meg-poag

Chapter 2: Copper "Comfort, Abundance, and Positivity"

Energy is Currency:

Hareesh. (2015). What Does 'Energy' Mean?. https://hareesh.org/blog/2015/9/23/what-does-energy-mean

Maroutian, E. (2024). Quotefancy. https://quotefancy.com/quote/2505041/Emily-Maroutian-Energy-is-the-currency-of-the-universe-When-you-pay-attention-to

Martinez, J. (2023). What is Spiritual Energy and Why Businesspeople should care about it. https://www.linkedin.com/pulse/what-spiritual-energy-why-businesspeople-should-care-martinez

Smil, V. (2024). Quotefancy. https://quotefancy.com/quote/1656787/Vaclav-Smil-Energy-is-the-only-universal-currency-one-of-its-many-forms-must-be

Vallis, B. (2021). All the different types of energy and how to harness them for your brightest day. https://www.rituals.com/en-us/mag-rituality-types-of-energy.html

Mental Peace:

Boutros, N., (2024). Inner Peace: Definition, Examples, & How to Find It. https://www.berkeleywellbeing.com/inner-peace.html

Chérif, L., Niemiec, R., & Wood, V. (2022). Character strengths and inner peace. International Journal of Wellbeing, 12(3).

Emerson, R., W. (2024). Goodreads. https://www.goodreads.com/quotes/38023-nothing-can-bring-you-peace-but-yourself-nothing-can-bring

Moore, C. (2019). How to Find Inner Peace and Happiness. https://positivepsychology.com/inner-peace-happiness/

Tolle, E. (2024). Goodreads. https://www.goodreads.com/quotes/47872-you-find-peace-not-by-rearranging-the-circumstances-of-your

Chapter 3: Blue "Truth, Emotional Depth, and Inner Peace"

Freedom of Truth:

Dewey, L. (2024). The Alchemy of Natural Healing: "I Remembered Who I Am" [Spoken Word Poem]. https://thealchemyofnatural-healing.buzzsprout.com/2311595/15043012-bonus-i-remembered-who-i-am-spoken-word-poem

Heidegger, M. (1943). On the Essence of Truth. https://aphelis.net/wp-content/uploads/2011/02/Martin-Heidegger-On-the-Essence-of-Truth.pdf

Lonscu, L. (2022). How Our Beliefs and Values Shape Our Behavior: A Beginner's Guide. https://iulianionescu.com/blog/how-our-beliefs-and-values-shape-our-behavior/

St. Maarten, A. (2024). Essence of Truth. Goodreads. https://www.goodreads.com/quotes/9795754-truth-has-a-power-only-the-courageous-can-handle

Wyatt, J. & Ulatowski, J. (2022). How to Think about Truth. Psyche Digital Magazine. https://psyche.co/guides/how-to-think-about-truth-in-a-philosophically-informed-way

Inner Silence:

Center for Action & Contemplation. (2020). Inner Silence. https://cac.org/daily-meditations/inner-silence-2020-01-08/

Rumi, (2024). Goodreads. https://www.goodreads.com/quotes/27617-silence-is-the-language-of-god-all-else-is-poor

Sri Sri Ravi Shankar, G. (2016). Art of Living. https://wisdom.srisriravishankar.org/inner-silence-is-the-source-of-intuition/

Tolle, E. (2003). Stillness Speaks. https://lifeintegrity.com/Eckhart-Tolle-Stillness-Speaks.pdf

Weaver, T. (2023). 20 Quotes on the Power of Silence: Chaim Potok Quote. https://orionphilosophy.com/quotes-on-silence/

Chapter 4: Gold "Divinity, Generosity, and Success"

Soul Responsibility:

Desai, T. (2021). The Human Consciousness, How Much We Know?. Medium. https://medium.com/illumination/the-human-consciousness-how-much-do-we-know-207b1535cbdf

Smith, J. (2024). Quotefancy. https://quotefancy.com/judah-smith-quotes

Smith, J. A. (2009). Aristotle: On the Soul. http://classics.mit.edu/Aristotle/soul.html

Spinks, M. (n.d.). The Responsibility of my Soul. https://library.timelesstruths.org/texts/The_Responsibility_of_My_Soul/The_Responsibility_of_My_Soul/

Nurturing your Internal Divinity:

Dyer, W. (2024). BrainQuote. https://www.brainyquote.com/quotes/wayne_dyer_718044

Mashburn, R. (2020). What Does it Mean 'The Spirit is Willing but the Flesh is Weak'?. https://www.christianity.com/wiki/bible/mean-the-spirit-is-willing-but-the-flesh-is-weak.html

Rahman, A. R. (2024). BrainQuote. https://www.brainyquote.com/quotes/a_r_rahman_623296

Turner, S. (n.d.). Embracing The Divine Feminine and Nurturing Your Inner Goddess. Nudian Impulse. https://www.nubianimpulse.com/post/embracing-the-divine-feminine-and-nurturing-your-inner-goddess

Wixom, R. M. (2015). Discovering the Divinity Within. https://www.churchofjesuschrist.org/study/general-conference/2015/10/discovering-the-divinity-within?lang=eng

Chapter 5: Red "Intention, Thought, and Victory"

Cogito, Ergo Sum: I Think, Therefore I am:

Einstein, A. (2024). Goodreads. https://www.goodreads.com/quotes/1799-the-world-as-we-have-created-it-is-a-process

John 6 (KJV). And Jesus said unto them,. https://www.blueletterbible.org/kjv/jhn/6/35/s_1003035

John 14 (KJV). Jesus saith unto him, I. https://www.blueletterbible.org/kjv/jhn/14/6/s_1011006

John 15 (KJV). Henceforth I call you not. https://www.blueletterbible.org/kjv/jhn/15/15/s_1012015

Lewis, R. (2023). What Actually is a Thought? And How Is Information Physical?. Psychology Today. https://www.psychologytoday.com/us/blog/finding-purpose/201902/what-actually-is-a-thought-and-how-is-information-physical

Maden, J. (2023). I Think Therefore I Am: Descartes' Cogito Ergo Sum Explained. https://philosophybreak.com/articles/i-think-therefore-i-am-descartes-cogito-ergo-sum-explained/

Miller, S. (2004). Disgust the Gatekeeper Emotion. The Analytic Press Inc.. https://books.google.com/books?id=91AGYNrUBDMC

Tracy, B. (2024). BrainyQuote. https://www.brainyquote.com/quotes/brian_tracy_385850

Battle of the Spirit:

Peterson, J. (n.d.). AZ Quotes. https://www.azquotes.com/quote/937340

Shinn, F. S. (2016). The Complete Works of Florence Scovel Shinn. Martino Fine Books. ISBN 978-1-68422-047-2

Stoyer, J. (2024). Goodreads. https://www.goodreads.com/author/quotes/7712974.June_Stoyer

Chapter 6: Orange "Creativity, Productivity, and Emotional Expression"

Human Nature and Emotional Intelligence:

Cherry, K. (2024). Emotional Intelligence: How We Perceive, Evaluate, Express, and Control Emotions. https://www.verywellmind.com/what-is-emotional-intelligence-2795423

Chopra, D. (2024). Quotefancy. https://quotefancy.com/quote/792692/Deepak-Chopra-When-emotional-intelligence-merges-with-spiritual-intelligence-human-nature

Grant, A. (2024). BrainyQuote. https://www.brainyquote.com/quotes/adam_grant_834184

Groeneveld, E. (2017). Homo Sapiens. https://www.worldhistory.org/Homo_Sapiens/#google_vignette

Meinch, T. (2023). What We Know about Homo Habilis. Discover Magazine. https://www.discovermagazine.com/the-sciences/what-we-know-about-homo-habilis

The Power of Words:

Capps, C. (2024). Goodreads. https://www.goodreads.com/quotes/744801-words-are-the-most-powerful-thing-in-the-universe-words

Prince, J. (2024). Joseph Prince's Devotional 'The Power of Your Words' Day 42. Life.Church. https://www.bible.com/reading-plans/28-joseph-prince/day/42

Proverbs 18 (KJV). Death and life [are] in. Retrieved from https://www.blueletterbible.org/kjv/pro/18/21/s_646021

Chapter 7: Green "Balance, Stability, and Energy"

CTRL + ALT + DEL: Balance of Emotions:

Alder, S. (2024). Quotefancy. https://quotefancy.com/shannon-l-alder-quotes

Hay, L. L. (2024). BrainyQuote. https://www.brainyquote.com/quotes/louise_l_hay_540610?src=t_balance

NHS Fife. (n.d.). Emotional Balance. https://www.nhsfife.org/services/all-services/child-and-adolescent-mental-health-service-camhs/things-to-try/emotional-balance/

Beta Brain Waves: Frequency of Thought:

Goleman, D. (2007). Emotional Intelligence (10th ed.). Bantam Books.

Herrmann, N. (1997). What is the Function of the Various Brain-waves?. Scientific American. https://www.scientificamerican.com/article/what-is-the-function-of-t-1997-12-22/

Hill, N. (2024). Quotefancy. https://quotefancy.com/quote/871162/Napoleon-Hill-Every-human-brain-is-both-a-broadcasting-and-receiving-station-for-the

Hills, K. (2022). Effective Leadership and the Practice of Emotional Intelligence. In Bansal, M.; Leyland, C. & Hills, K. (Eds.). Multi-Disciplinary Perspectives in Thought Leadership. (pp. 27-32). Lambert Academic Publishing.

Kotsos, T. (2021). Brainwaves & Consciousness: Understanding Brainwave Frequencies. Mind your Reality. https://mind-your-reality.com/brainwaves.html

Meda, K. (2020). How to Manipulate Brain Waves for a Better Mental State. https://www.jeffersonhealth.org/your-health/living-well/how-to-manipulate-brain-waves-for-a-better-mental-state

Voltaire. (2024). Goodreads. https://www.goodreads.com/quotes/51535-the-human-brain-is-a-complex-organ-with-the-wonderful

Chapter 8: Silver "Evolution, Gratitude, and Consciousness"

Human Consciousness: The Idea of Self- Awareness:

Ashby, M. (2024). Muata Ashby Quotes. Bookroo. https://bookroo.com/quotes/muata-ashby

Biswas-Diener, R. & Teeny, J. (2024). States of consciousness. In R. Biswas-Diener & E. Diener (Eds), Noba textbook series: Psychology. Champaign, IL: DEF publishers. Retrieved from http://noba.to/xj2cbhek

Cherry, K. (2023). Consciousness in Psychology. https://www.verywell-mind.com/what-is-consciousness-2795922

Chowdhury, A. (2023). What is Consciousness? https://www.linkedin.com/pulse/what-consciousness-anup-chowdhury-

Robbins, T. (2024). Goodreads. https://www.goodreads.com/quotes/74657-our-great-human-adventure-is-the-evolution-of-conscious-ness-we

Thrineshwara, M.R. (2018). Understanding the Difference Between Consciousness and Awareness. https://www.linkedin.com/pulse/understanding-difference-between-consciousness-awareness-m-r

Voice of America. (2023). Awareness vs. Consciousness. https://learnin-genglish.voanews.com/a/awareness-vs-consciousness-/7268223.html

Spiritual Evolution, Gratitude, and Growth:

Beattie, M. (2024). PassItOn. https://www.passiton.com/inspirational-quotes/7164-gratitude-unlocks-the-fullness-of-life-it

Gordan-Mead, W. (2023). Spiritual Evolution: How to Experience your True Nature. https://whitneygordon-mead.medium.com/spiritual-evolution-how-to-experience-your-true-nature-727bbc15eff5

Kang, J. C. (2015). Spirituality of Gratitude. IVP.

Tolle, E. (2024). BrainQuote. https://www.brainyquote.com/quotes/eckhart_tolle_571604

Chapter 9: Purple "Manifestation, Imagination, and Universal Flow"

The Power of Manifestation:

Boomplay. (2023, March 15). Is Manifestation in the Bible? [Podcast]. Episode 54. https://www.boomplay.com/podcasts/95049

Coelho, P. (2014). The Alchemist. HarperOne.

Davis, T. (2023). What Is Manifestation? Science-Based Ways to Manifest. Psychology Today. https://www.psychologytoday.com/us/blog/click-here-for-happiness/202009/what-is-manifestation-science-based-ways-to-manifest

Flenory, D. & Flenory, T. (2021, September 26). BMF: Season 1, Episode 1. https://www.imdb.com/title/tt13806618/

Lazor, T. (2022). Manifestation: What Does the Bible Say About It?. Watermark Community Church. https://www.watermark.org/blog/manifestation

Scott, W. D. (1908). The laws of progressive thinking. Small, Maynard & Company. (pp. 147–156). https://doi.org/10.1037/13645-011

Tarrants, T. A. (2019). Biblical Meditation. C.S. Lewis Institute. https://www.cslewisinstitute.org/wp-content/uploads/KD-2019-Winter-Biblical-Meditation-7556.pdf

Imagination: The Superpower of Storytelling:

2 Corinthians 10 (KJV). Casting down imaginations, and every. Retrieved from https://www.blueletterbible.org/kjv/2co/10/5/s_1088005

Ballard, J. G. (2024). Goodreads. https://www.goodreads.com/quotes/42220-i-believe-in-the-power-of-the-imagination-to-remake

Bodo, V. (2023). Consciousness and Imagination. Medium. https://medium.com/@dr.victor.bodo/consciousness-and-imagination-60395c846c22

Gosetti-Ferencei, J. (2023). 'Imagination in human evolution', Imagination: A Very Short Introduction, Very Short Introductions. Oxford Academic. https://doi.org/10.1093/actrade/9780198830023.003.0002

Hurston, Z. N. (n.d.). 30 Best Zora Neale Hurston Quotes. Bookey. https://www.bookey.app/quote-author/zora-neale-hurston

Serrat, O. (2008). Storytelling. Knowledge Solutions. https://www.adb.org/sites/default/files/publication/27637/story-telling.pdf

St. Aubin, D. (2021). Real Faith, Real Life: Dare to Imagine. https://doverfirst.org/media/yj5x4dk/real-faith-real-life-dare-to-imagine

www.ingramcontent.com/pod-product-compliance
Lightning Source LLC
Chambersburg PA
CBHW051250150726
48001CB00019B/2178